God Uses
An Ignorant And
Unlearned Man

James Fox

Venice Roper

ISBN 978-1-63525-789-2 (Paperback)
ISBN 978-1-63525-790-8 (Digital)

Christian Faith Publishing, Inc.
296 Chestnut Street
Meadville, PA 16335
www.christianfaithpublishing.com

Printed in the United States of America

FOREWORD

The story you are about to read could be hard to believe. Can these things be so? Can God really use "an unlearned and ignorant man" as Jim Fox describes himself?

I had no idea when I sat across from Jim at a pastor's prayer gathering what God had in mind but I am delighted to have been a part of Jim's journey. At the time of this writing, I have served as the lead evangelist for an Outpouring of the Spirit at a church in Terre Haute, IN since August of 2010. For me one of the most significant things in this Outpouring has been the transformation in the lives and ministries of preachers who "had been with Jesus" (Acts 4:13). This small book tells one of those stories.

I have watched God use Jim and Tana, not only in the Outpouring, but also in other nations where they have travelled with us.

Prophets of the Old Testament often became the sign and wonder. In a somewhat similar way Jim and Tana Fox have become a sign and a wonder. In spite of broken marriages, broken ministry, and broken relationships God has used them to bring healing and hope to others.

As I read the pages of this story I was reminded of the verse of Scripture in 1 Corinthians 10:11, "Now all these things happened unto them for ensamples: and they are written for our admonition, upon whom the ends of the world are come." I am aware the passage I just quoted is a revelation of God's purpose for the Old Testament. However, I do not think I do an injustice to say God has done these things in the life of Jim and Tana to be an example...to encourage other "unlearned and ignorant" (Acts 4:13) people. There is a line in a great song that says, "it is no secret what God can do, what He has done for others He can do for you."

As I read this account my own heart ached anew to see even more of His Glory and power demonstrated so that others "might believe that Jesus is the Christ, the Son of God; and that believing ye might have life through his name" (John 20:31).

Thanks Jim and Tana for sharing this part of the journey. I encourage you to keep on walking obediently as unlearned and ignorant people. Surely the best is yet to come.

MICHAEL LIVENGOOD
EVANGELIST and AUTHOR of "THE GLORY FACTOR"
published by Evergreen Press
mikliven@aol.com
www.mikelivengoodministries.com

Jim Fox has written a book that will enlarge your faith in God and release a very powerful challenge to pursue more of Him.

This book is a testimony of Gods mega Grace and provision on the path of His leading as Jim and Tana constantly step into the increase of Gods Outpouring.

You will be blessed, motivated and encouraged to stay to the task God has planned for your life as you read God Uses an Ignorant and Unlearned Man.

Keith E. Taylor
Senior Pastor Cross Tabernacle Church and CEO of Gilgal Ministries

I have known Jim for six years and over that time I have watched him wrestle with the things that life has thrown up at him. He has come through with Flying colours. This book is the Autobiography of a man who is the real deal. Life is not always fair, and unlike a lot of people that I have met Jim has maintained a Christ like spirit and a thankful heart through all the trials of life that he has walked through. This book will give you hope and courage, it will encourage you to press on into the things that God has in store for you. And will help you to stand in the trials of your faith knowing that God is always working for your good and his glory in all we do no matter what the world may throw at us providing we continue to walk according to his purposes. You will be blessed and encouraged as you read this account of a simple man with a simple faith putting his trust in God which enables him to continue to do great and mighty things for the kingdom.

Yours in Christ Graham Renouf

MY BEGINNING YEARS

THIS IS A BIOGRAPHY OF me, Jim Fox. My given name is James Edwin Fox. I was Born in Terre Haute, Indiana, on November 18, 1953, to Charles (Charlie) and Marcella (Marcy) Fox. I have one sister, Sondra (Sonnie), born January 25, 1949. I was raised for a year and half at Twelfth and Putnam in Terre Haute, Indiana; then, we moved to rural Farmersburg, Indiana, very close to where my Dad was born and raised. At age five, we moved again one mile south of where we were, into a house my uncle lived in. It had been a parsonage for Nyes Chapel Church, which sat straight across the road from the house with a cemetery next to it. My Dad worked in Terre Haute, Indiana, at Wabash Fiber Box Company for forty-four years and, as far as I know, didn't miss but a handful of days in all those years. Dad was a good provider for his family; we always had what we needed. I had a good childhood, very normal in most ways for living in the sticks of rural Indiana. Dad taught me how to fish, hunt, and how to make my way through the woods. I loved sports; I got that from my Mom. When I was young, baseball was my life, and I was good at it. The two brothers down the road north of us were good too, probably better than me, but I wouldn't admit it. We pushed each other to become the best we could be in every sport we knew how to play. Half a mile to the east lived two girls that I had great affection for and still pray for every day. My dad's mom and dad lived west of us across the cornfields about a half a mile away. They were Jesse and Mae Fox. I am sure they prayed me into the kingdom and my preaching heritage originated from them.

I spent a lot of time by myself. With my sister being five years older than me and no one living real close, I just did things by myself. My first encounters with God came through my grandparents as I would spend time with them, especially when my cousins would come to visit. Grandpa read his Bible every night and got on his knees to pray before he went to bed. They took me to the church across the road from where I lived, when I would let them. I had some neighbors that took me to Bible school each summer when I was in junior high and that was how I was first introduced to the gospel. Little did I know what Father had in store for this ignorant, unlearned young man.

During my high school years, I don't remember going to church at all, but I wasn't one to get in trouble or at least get caught. I didn't have close friends but knew everyone. I dated some, not a lot, desiring to have a relationship with a girl. I had a fairly good high school experience, made A's and B's and some C's, but overall did OK. I started putting up hay when I was a freshman and was mowing the grass in the cemetery across the road. Then, when I turned sixteen, I bought my first car, a 1953 Chevy Belaire for twenty-five dollars, and it ran good. My next car was a 1964

Ford Galaxy. By this time, I was working in my sister and brother-in-law's gas station. I was just an average young man going to school and working. I graduated from high school at the age of seventeen in May of 1971.

When I started working a lot, I also started experimenting with smoking. I couldn't handle the smoke, so I never did do that. I would never chew; that was just too nasty. And drugs were never an option with me, so I started doing some drinking—not a lot just when I thought I could get away with it. Dad always liked drinking beer and spent time with friends at the tavern playing cards and drinking beer. This meant I was around it at home, but I didn't like the taste of beer. So I would drink brandy and wine when I could get it; to me, that was cool, and it tasted better.

I decided when I got out of high school I wanted to go to electronics school. This didn't settle with my dad; he thought I should just get a good job in a factory and be happy like him. I didn't. I went off to school in Louisville, Kentucky, at the United Electronics Institute, a two-year, year-round school. What a culture shock that was; I went to school for twenty hours a week and worked forty hours a week to pay for everything. I started drinking and partying regularly and lasted about nine months before I flunked out and had to come home. When I did, I admitted defeat and got a job in the factory where my Dad worked.

I started running around with a cousin, and we had a friend that would buy us whatever we wanted. Both of us were sneaky and lied about everything. My cousin was better at that than I was, but I could curse better than him. We decided to start looking for girls, and the best place we could think of was in a church. That would be better than most places we had been. I ended up introducing him to a girl I graduated with, and they did get married—the best thing that ever happen to the boy except for Jesus. I started spending time with her sister and the youth group she was involved with. My cousin and I had told so many lies and had even come to church drunk. We told everyone we were saved and put on a good front—we thought. But the time had come that I was going to face the truth.

SALVATION AND
MY FIRST STEPS

IN APRIL OF 1973, THIS little church I was going to—so I could be with this girl—decided to have a revival, a weeklong revival. Since I had already told everyone that I was saved, I just went to be with the girl. I couldn't tell you much about what went on the whole week; I didn't pay too much attention to what was happening but did enjoy the singing, and several gave their hearts to Jesus. Then, on the last night of the revival (which was Friday night and it happened to be Good Friday), they decided to take all the ones who had accepted Jesus to another church in another town and baptize them, so all of us went to watch them get dunked. I don't remember ever witnessing a water baptism before. This was a big church, and it was after our church service—later in the evening, around ten, ten-thirty. I sat there, watching each of them confess Jesus as their Lord and Savior, then they would lower them into the water; and they would come up almost glowing. I was feeling really weird inside and didn't know what was going on. When the preacher was done with the last one, he asked us all to stand I was hanging on to the pew in front of me with a death grip, white knuckles and all. Then, he said, "Is there anyone else out there that would like to do what these have done and give their heart, soul, and body to Jesus and accept him as their Lord and Savior?"

This incredible sense of love, conviction, peace, guilt, joy, sorrow, and clean yet dirty feeling came upon me. My spirit knew it needed to respond, yet my flesh was fighting it with all it had. I found myself stepping into the isle and crying, saying I want that. I don't remember much between that and when I was getting ready to step into the baptistery, but when I stepped into the water, I felt a presence never before had I experienced. Then, I confessed my sins, received Jesus by faith as my Savior and Lord, and was baptized in water. I knew that I was saved by faith and that water baptism was an act of obedience and a sign of death, burial, and resurrection into Christ. When I came up out of the water, I was different. I didn't know just how much different until later. I was so happy, at peace, full of joy, and had zeal to want to tell everyone what had just happened. I was a changed person; instantly, I became a fanatic for Jesus. A transformation took place at that very moment; I lost all desire for alcohol, stopped using foul language, and didn't ever want to lie again. I had a terrible problem with anger, and Father took that away instantly. Now, I still had plenty of issues to deal with, but God was so good to me and set me free from many bondages. I was one changed dude.

At that moment, I knew I was to preach and wanted anything God had for me. My relationship with the girl I was seeing didn't last very long after this; the change in me was drastic, maybe too much for her. But I didn't let that discourage me; I pressed in toward God. I wanted to learn as much as I could about the Word of God so much, so that in a few months, they let me teach a Sunday school class; and within nine months, I preached my first sermon at a poor folks home in Sullivan, Indiana. It took about ten minutes, and I preached on love out of 1 Corinthians chapter 13. When elections for officers in the church came around at the beginning of the year, they put me in as a deacon. Not good. I took the position very seriously and started studying in 1 Timothy 3:8–16 about what a deacon was to be and act. I knew I didn't qualify for this and went to the leadership of the church to ask questions. I never got any answers; they told me I would do just fine and not to worry about it. The church was very small, and they were excited to have a new young man interested in serving the Lord. So I quit asking questions and started trying to answer my questions with the Word of God. This made me study even more, and before long, I found that although these were loving, caring people, they didn't know the Word of God.

There were other young ladies in the church, and a couple of them were interested in me and I in them. We had a good size group of young people that were active when I received Jesus; and then the pastor left, and most of the youth left the church. By this time, I was dating one of the young ladies in the church. She was a very possessive type; this should have told me to be careful, but infatuation is a blinder and a trap of the enemy.

When the pastor and young people left, the church needed someone to fill in to work with the young kids in the church, so I started a youth group. My personality was fitting for this, and the kids liked me. We didn't have church service on Sunday night, so we had youth group on Sunday evenings. Father started really blessing that group, and a lot of kids were ministered to during this time period. Within two years, we saw at least forty-five kids get saved and water baptized everyone one of them. You see, the group grew to about sixty, but there were only about thirty-five to forty in church on Sunday morning. This created a problem, and I was about to learn a lesson that I would never forget. But before I get into that, I made a big decision that would shape the rest of my life. I was getting married.

I GOT MARRIED AND MORE

I HAD STARTED DATING A very young girl. She was three years younger than me, the youngest of eight children, who was born with a heart condition and pretty much got anything she wanted. Her father had died before I met her, and her older brothers were trying to make up for her loss. I almost walked away from the relationship at one point in time but decided not to. We tried really hard to follow the Bible and restrained from having a total intimate relationship until we got married, but that didn't stop us from having other types of physical contact. As I said earlier, I still had issues to deal with and sex was one of them. But through it all, we were still virgins when we got married. She was very possessive and jealous, but that didn't matter to me at the time. I couldn't see where that would have any effect on our relationship. Oh, I forgot to mention she loved owning animals of all kinds.

Shortly after, I turned twenty-one and she turned eighteen, and we got married in February of 1975. We had a big church wedding and were the pride of the church. I found out on my wedding night she didn't want to have a total intimate relationship because she was afraid it would hurt, and she didn't want to get pregnant. Other than that, things seemed to be going well, and life was good. We still ran the youth group; I was active in lots of areas of the church and growing in the Lord by leaps and bounds. We had a group of young people we took to churches and ministered with, ministered to several youth in the town we were in, and were seeing them come to the Lord. Then, came the lesson I told you I was going to learn.

The elders of the church, although they liked having the youth there, started questioning why the parents of these kids were not coming. So they held a church meeting on a Sunday night while the kids were there and started questioning, in front of the kids, why they didn't get their parents to come to church. It was devastating to the kids and to us and ultimately destroyed the youth group. Father showed me in 1 Timothy 4:12 not to let no man despise thy youth but be an example of the believers, so I knew I had to leave. I could no longer be a part of that. I would never forget the attitude and lack of love. I just could not understand how people, Christian people, could treat kids that way. I never lost my belief in God, but my faith in people was shaken.

Life had gotten interesting. By this time we owned seven dogs, cats, a sheep, two goats, horses, a bird, and a ferret. She only wanted to be around her family for everything and never wanted to be around mine. The jealousy problem had become an issue, and the intimate relationship had grown even worse. I turned to being busy physically by training for triathlons. But that didn't help with my wondering eyes. Not that it was an excuse but the worse the jealousy got, the more I looked where I shouldn't be looking. With my factory job laying me off, it caused problems, although she didn't want me going to work. She wanted me right at home all the time. Through all this, I was still growing closer to God.

RECEIVING BAPTISM IN HOLY SPIRIT

FIVE YEARS INTO OUR MARRIAGE, we had been to a couple of different churches and had ended up in a little country church several miles from where we lived. There were a lot of young couples, and we were able to start helping with the youth. I seemed to always be interested in the youth. There was an older couple that we got close to, and they invited us to go out to eat. It was a Full Gospel Business Men's meeting with a special speaker. I was so hungry for more of God and was ready to do anything to get closer to him. Now the church I accepted Jesus as my Savior didn't believe in speaking in tongues; they said that stuff was of the devil and didn't exist in today's church. I didn't really understand a lot about being Spirit filled, but if it meant I could get closer to God, then bring it on. Acts chapter 2 was very plain about being Spirit filled, and many other places made me question the teaching I had received when I first got saved. We went with them, and what a night it was. I answered the altar call; the next thing I knew, I was laying on my back, speaking words that sounded funny. I had never seen someone slain in the Spirit, and this tongues thing was new. But I knew it was from God, and I wasn't going to let go. I was so afraid I would lose my new language that I memorized it. I didn't realize it came from the heart not the mind. For the next three weeks, I went around repeating the same short phrase. Then, at the end of three weeks, it was like God took my tongue and turned it loose on both ends. I started speaking in all these different types of languages and didn't want to stop. No one could ever tell me otherwise. This was a God thing; and as far as I was concerned, everyone needed this, and I was going to make sure they had the opportunity to receive it.

For the next eighteen months, this same couple brought couples to this meeting, and forty-five received the baptism in Holy Ghost. By this time, the little country church decided enough is enough and asked all of us to leave or stop speaking in tongues. This would make it the third church I had to leave.

FIRST YEARS OF MINISTRY

AS MENTIONED IN THE OTHER chapters, I began ministering shortly after I received Jesus as my Savior—filling in when needed, taking young people around to churches, singing and putting on skits, teaching Sunday school and youth groups. This continued everywhere I went; and after I received the baptism in Holy Ghost, there was a fire in me, and I would preach at the drop of a hat. In 2 Timothy 4:2, Father showed me to be ready to preach, in season and out. I had noticed that I seemed to be able to pick up on things about people; and I would know things before they happened, but I had no idea what that was all about at the time. I went to several different churches around the area, even married and buried some. I saw many receive Jesus, and that was exciting. But it always seemed there should be more. In 1985, I was asked by a pastor friend to hold a revival. It was scheduled for one week but went for two full weeks. This was a tremendous time of ministry. We saw all nine gifts that are talked about in 1 Corinthians 12:8–12 in action during that set of meetings. One young man that I had worked with had been in a factory accident that messed up his insides really bad. Father totally healed him; it was one of the first of many miracles I would witness. By this time, I was speaking into peoples' lives by giving words of the Lord to them, actively operating in the gifts of the Spirit, especially words of knowledge, words of wisdom and prophesy. Discernment, gifts of tongues, and interpretation of tongues was common. Gift of healings and the Gift of faith seemed to manifest every so often. But the gift of miracles just alluded me. I ministered from 1973 to 1988. But from 1980, 1988 was my busiest time of evangelism, preaching and holding revivals in many churches and a variety of denominations all over west central Indiana. I was ministering in the only way I knew how and knowing all along there was more, but I just didn't know how to get to it. Remember I didn't have any training, schooling, and no one to help me, so I did what I read in the Bible: "Study to show thyself approved" (2 Tim. 2:15) and "do the work of an evangelist" (2 Tim. 4:5." Then, came the fall.

THE FALL AND RESTORATION

BY 1987, I WAS LICENSED and ordained and still hungry for more of God. But my home life was miserable, and things had only gotten worse as far as the situation in my relationship with my wife was concerned. No need to go into any details—I just made some wrong decisions and had an affair with another woman. We had started a ministry with horses. My wife loved horses and no matter what we were going to have horses. I didn't really like horses, but that is the way it goes sometimes. It ended up with one of the couples that joined the horse club having trouble in their marriage, and things went too far.

By the time everything was exposed, I realized I had no affection for my wife. I was miserable in my situation, and in my mind, there was no way out. I left and filed for divorce. The woman, my future wife, had already left her husband because of mental problems and threats to kill himself and her. The move I made meant that I lost my license and ordination. I was also asked to leave the church I was in. I knew at this time my ministry was over, and all I would ever do from here on was just be a pew sitter and maybe help out doing things around the church. The sad part was I thought that was better than spending the rest of my life living a lie and being miserable. I lost everything, just walked away, and went back to live at my mom and dad's—no car, no church, no wife, no other woman. I did still have a job, so I started looking for a church. I looked around, and then, after a period of time, the other woman invited me to a church that her and a man she was dating was going to. So I went, and the first Sunday I was there, the pastor spoke into my life. I realized maybe there was life on the other side of sin and divorce that had never been told to me before. But how do you get to it, and what does it take?

I thought I had already repented and asked forgiveness, but what I did not understand was the process of restoration. I counseled with the pastor and started being restored into the body of Christ. The other woman had stopped seeing the man she was with and also started restoration. The pastor started using us in small positions, and our relationship was rekindled the right way this time. This went on for about a year; it came time for us to decide what we wanted to do. On to a new adventure.

GOD'S SECOND-CHANCE PROVISION

THE OTHER WOMAN'S NAME WAS Tana; we became very close on a different level and started spending a lot of time together, doing the work of the Lord. Through counseling, repentance, forgiveness, and time seeking Father, we started seeing that although we had made some majors mistakes, there was still a place in the kingdom of God for us and that we could move on to fulfill our purpose that Father had designed us to do. We had not committed the unpardonable sin; we could be forgiven, and Father still wanted to use us in our callings. "The gifts and calling of God are without repentance" (Rom. 11:29). Father had told me that if I didn't do it his way, it would take years to recover from my mistakes. So I settled in to the idea that I would be whatever he wanted me to be and do whatever he wanted me to do.

I had started doing construction work, and things were going pretty good. Tana was working at a hardware supply store, so we were in good shape that way. During the summer after the divorce, I did a lot of ministering on the streets and started bringing several of the inner-city people to church. Finally, after being counseled, we decided to get married. And on November 17, 1989, we tied the knot. Except for my encounters with God, this was one of the happiest days of my life. We had a great honeymoon in Gatlinburg, Tennessee, at a conference with some well-known ministers. Our marriage was off to a great start, and we were both thankful and overwhelmed at what Father had done for us even through all the mistakes. With a repentant heart and being washed in the blood of Jesus and our sins being forgiven, we had a second chance, and I wasn't about to blow it this time.

By this time, I was doing a lot of ministering, and being used in the pulpit, I was being asked to minister in other churches. You see, my second chance also included being restored back to where I was before my fall. Only Father in heaven can put you back where you came from, but I had a long way to go because I had to pay the price for what I had done. In February of 1990, Tana's mom died very suddenly. In March, we had plans to go to the Philippines and Thailand on a mission's trip; we went ahead with our plans. We traveled with four other people; one of which had the contacts and was able to get us into places to minister. Remember we are still dealing with the idea of God's second chance. I had never flown on a large plane before, and at thirty-six years of age, it was a wonderful experience. I had never seen the ocean before; both happened in the same day. After five airplanes, we landed in Manila, Philippines. What a culture shock. Men were holding machine guns in the airport. The smell was terrible. It was dark, and we got our first ride in the traffic; we weren't in Indiana anymore. We stayed in the Philippines for two weeks, then went to Thailand for two weeks, then back to the Philippines for two more weeks. What a trip. In the Philippines, we got to minister in several different churches, home groups, and camp meetings. In Thailand, we were ministering to those training for the ministry and got to go into the mountains and stay a night in one of the villages. We traveled all over Thailand and got to see most of that country. Life changing to say the least, but the one thing that showed me Father was still willing to use me was the manifestation of miracles—something not seen in the States. During the six weeks we were gone, we saw cancers and lungs healed. Father even raised one lady from the dead. Plus many were delivered from demons, one had over fifty in her. What a wonderful experience. There were many who received Jesus, and the prophetic flowed with ease. Father was still able to use this ignorant and unlearned man because I had never seen the miraculous move like this before, and it made me understand that restoration had taken place. Father had placed his wayward son back into the body, but would God's children be as willing to do so? The second chance from God was sealed; all that was needed to be done was to follow him every day. While we were in Thailand, a pastor prophesied over us that we would have a son. Well, at age thirty-seven and thirty-six, Tana and I just couldn't see how that would happen and thought he was a little off. I was ready to go into fulltime ministry and didn't have time for a family this late in life. Then, we went home, and the ministry began. Smooth sailing from here on out, I thought.

EXIT STAGE
RIGHT RESTORATION
INTO THE WILDERNESS

WE CAME BACK FROM OUR trip and hit the ground running. Ministry was flowing, and things were looking good. We were in church about six days a week; I was teaching what they call a college-level course in a school our pastor had set up. We were youth pastors, elders, and the go-to guys for anything that needed to be done in ministry. I was seeing people come to Jesus; we didn't stress baptism in Holy Ghost too much, and every so often, someone might get healed. The presence of God would show up and had some powerful services. But where were the signs, wonders, and miracles? We had a set of services that was a turning point for the church, a mighty move of God. The pastor had meetings he was going to and shut our meeting down. Only to realize later it was a mistake. In September of 1992, our pastor called all of us to go on a fast—as long as we could—and challenged us, with him, on a forty-day fast. So I did, and that experience changed me more than I could have ever dreamed it would, bringing me to a whole new relationship with my Heavenly Father. I would go on to do two more forty-day fasts in the future, fasting became a huge part of my life.

Then, in November 1992, a prophetess and a psalmist came to our little church. The prophetess prophesied in rhyme, and the psalmist played in the Spirit the whole time. She gave a Word of the Lord over Tana and I that would prove to be the lifeblood of our relationship with Father and get us through the wilderness. Part of that Word was that Tana and I would dance before the Lord and bring the dance back into the church—not a dance of beauty and grace but of power and authority, the dance of the warrior. In Psalm 149:3 and 150:4, it tells us to dance in praise. Without knowing anything about us and not knowing our names, especially our last name, she prophesied and called us little foxes: "Foxes that have been made to run not go amuck. This is the night that God says he will ignite the tail of the little foxes. And they will run ablaze, giving glory to the ancient of days. And you shall run through wheat that is very, very dry, and you shall ignite it with the fire that shall be seen in the sky. Those men and women that have been cold in their seat—you're going to run Foxes of Fire." We use this name for the ministry. What an experience and blessing beyond anything we could imagine at the time.

Then, came the price I had to pay—just when we thought everything was getting better and better and we were on our way to full time ministry, nothing holding us back. I was licensed again; it was looking good, then all hell broke loose. In January of 1993, our pastors came back from a convention. We were sitting with them, telling them the things that had went on while they were gone.

Because of something that was said, not something we had done, the pastor's wife blew up at us and accused us of all kinds of things that were not true. It had to be one of the most terrible moments in my life, and we had literally done nothing; but there was no talking to her about it. We had just taken on another year as youth pastors and had other obligations in the church, so what were we to do. We prayed about it, and Father said to stay where we were. You see, when you joined this church, you took on a covenant with the church and the pastors, an agreement that was not to be broken by either party; and by this time, I had learned a lot about covenant. It was the subject I taught in the minister's school. Well, it was like this. I had been asked to leave or told I didn't belong in five churches because of many different reasons, with the only one that was truly my fault was when I had my fall, so I wasn't about to make a mistake this time. I didn't want to mess up my second chance no matter what I had to go through. So we stayed. The pastor was also bound by the covenant agreement, and he was willing to wait it out. He did everything to get us to leave. From the pulpit he called us leapers, Absolons and said for no one to fellowship with us. We fulfilled our duty in the responsibilities we had that year and asked Father if we could leave, and he said no; so we set for another year. The glorious ministry we thought was right at our fingertips was gone. Everything we had seen restored vanished into thin air, and as far as we could see, we hadn't done anything wrong. I was beginning to see the price I was to pay for what I had done. It didn't come in the way I was expecting it, but I knew Father had to show me some things and walk me through some tough times to see if I was really going to stick it out with him. I had to make some hard decisions. We held on to the prophetic word spoken to us and knew Father would get us through.

BLESSINGS IN
THE MIDST OF TURMOIL

JUST LIKE THE CHILDREN OF Israel who had everything they needed and lacked nothing but were in the wilderness, so was it with Tana and I. We were being persecuted by those we had trusted and believed in, yet Father was preparing us for what was coming; and we couldn't see. By the time we got close to the end of the first year of the persecution, Father started talking to me about a lot of things. And one day, while I was on a job site (by this time, I had developed my own business and was doing well), he spoke to me so plainly and told me that I was to have a son.

Now let me back up just a little and explain that Tana and I had talked this over and for us to have a baby at this point in time was risky, and at age thirty-nine how would we ever keep up with a child? And we would be sixty years old by the time he graduated. So I thought in my mind Tana is not going to go for this, and this cannot be God; so I tried to put it out of my mind. Now, remember in 1990, it was spoken to us we were going to have a son, and now, Father is speaking to me to have a son. Then came the truth. Tana showed up at my workplace and brought me lunch, so I thought I will just put this to rest right now. I explained to her what Father had been talking to me about, and I just knew it couldn't be him. Before I could get done talking, Tana started crying and sobbing. She said, "I knew what we had decided on, but I wanted a baby so bad. And I was afraid to say anything because I knew how you felt, and now Father has talked to you." Well, by this time, I was in shock. My mouth was open, and I didn't know what to say and was afraid to say anything. So we set and cried together and talked things out as to what this would mean and what we would have to do and came to the conclusion that if we were going to be obedient, we had to do what Father wanted us to do. Remember, we were in the midst of all the turmoil at the church we are attending, but at home, things were hoping pretty good.

In August of 1994, my mom and dad decided to take a trip to Minnesota—where my mom was raised—and wanted to take my sister, Tana, and myself along. So all of us went and had a great time. While we are gone, Tana got sick on some food and wasn't feeling normal. When we got home, we found out she was pregnant.

Now in 1993, because we were no longer as busy in the ministry and because of what the prophetess had spoken to us, our lives had taken a new twist. When we were told to bring the dance of the warrior back to the church, I just couldn't see how that would happen, so we went to prayer. Father told me to go study martial arts. Well, when I received Jesus as my Savior, the church I was attending said that was of the devil and no one should be involved in it. I knew this could not be God. But the more we prayed, the louder Father spoke about studying martial arts. We then went to the library to find out the history behind martial arts. We came to find out most martial arts are based on some type of religion but not all. There were some that were studied for military use only. So we went and found a martial arts school that taught one of those styles. The instructor turned out to be a distant relative of Tana's. We explained what we were there for, and he had no problem with it and welcomed us. This was part of what we occupied our time since we were no longer going to church so much.

Now it was August of 1994. We were studying martial arts and were busy in the construction business. Tana was pregnant with what we knew was a baby boy. The pregnancy was a breeze; Tana was helping me put siding on a house, was doing all the doctor would let her do in martial arts class, and was feeling great. Things were looking terrific in that area, and our church life was also just about to take a turn.

OUT OF THE FRYING PAN INTO THE FIRE

WE HAD BEEN LOOKING FOR another church; we knew we would be leaving but just didn't know when or how. Tana's aunt and uncle were pastors of a small congregation in the northern part of town and had been talking to us about coming there to help them in that work. But we had not been released by Father from the church we were at. In January of 1995, the church we were attending changed the name of the church, and Father said, "Now, you can leave for your obligation is fulfilled to the church you were in covenant with." Praise God, glory hallelujah—the door was opened, and it was time to leave. Now, in my life, this had been the sixth church I had been either asked to leave or told I didn't belong. But this time, I felt like I had tried to leave by the direction of God and not in the way of the flesh. For two years, we set and took the verbal abuse and accusations with no retaliation. Not bragging on me, but that was one lesson I didn't intend to have to learn again. So on to our next adventure, a new church with a lot of family in charge.

We seemed to fit in and the people were loving and everybody was excited about Tana getting ready to have a baby. We were the greatest thing that had happened to this little church since the discovery of popcorn. We stepped right in and started helping in areas they had need of. Excitement was in us that we could minister, and a bright future was in front of us again after two years of being shoved to the side. Our construction business was going well; we were enjoying church again and were just about to have a baby. Well, we didn't even pick a girl's name because we knew it was going to be a boy. Tana was feeling great; things were all coming together. Life was good.

About three weeks from the time the baby was to be here, Tana started having a headache. I was on a job site out in the country, northeast of town. Tana was taking care of some business with her dad, and the headache just kept getting worse. She called the doctor. He wanted to see her, so she went into the office. They checked her out and said you are going to go to the hospital. They called me and told me what was going on, so I took off. When I got to the hospital, Tana had not been there very long. They were taking blood, checking everything, and waiting for the test results to come back. We were sitting there, joking around, and I noticed her blood pressure was 221 over 107. I asked the nurse, in my ignorance, if that was a little high. The nurse quickly told me to be quiet and stepped out of the room. By this time, I knew something wasn't right but had no idea what. They soon got the results of the test, and Tana's body was rejecting the baby. She had gone from toxsima to preeclampsia. Her kidneys and other organs were beginning to shut down, and she could go into shock any moment. They told me to stay out of the way. They were going to have to take the baby, so I had to run down the hall to keep up with them, kiss her right before they went into the emergency room. And she was out of sight. Five minutes later, they brought out to me this perfect little baby boy; everything was all right with him, only he didn't have any baby fat. But he was healthy. Tana, however, wasn't doing so well. Her entire body was swollen from fluids; the blood vessels in her eyes had burst, so she couldn't see. And her whole body was a mess. They told us that in a matter of minutes, both of them could have died. I came that close to losing them both, but Father had purpose for both of them. Jesse was doing fine, but Tana had a long recovery and was in the hospital for four days. She wanted so desperately to breastfeed, but with what her body went through, she couldn't produce milk. It was at least a week before her eyes cleared up, so she could see what her baby looked like.

Oh, we named him Jesse Ezra Fox—after the biblical person, my grandfather, and Tana's great-grandfather. The middle name was to fit the man of God he was to become. It was a very frustrating and emotional time for Tana, trying to recover from the surgery and all the aftereffects she went through. With time, she started bouncing back, slow but sure. We continued to work in the church, and the church was growing. We had started a food pantry; God was blessing us, so we were blessing the church. Things were going great. Then, by January of 1996, we found out Jesse was going to have a sibling. We knew it was going to be a girl, and the excitement started all over again.

In the beginning of March, Tana miscarried, and our world was rocked. What was God doing? Why did this happen? Why didn't he answer our prayers? We had never known what losing a child was like nor did we realize that a miscarriage was the same as a death. It was devastating to say the least. By this time, Tana was not her normal self physically—after everything she had been through in the last year—and wondered if she would ever get back to normal. As we were recovering from that loss, Father was still moving, and we set our sights on raising Jesse and ministering more. Just never give up on the promises of God, for he is faithful and true to carry them out no matter your education or the mistakes you have made. Through repentance and forgiveness, I was being washed in the blood of my Savior and Lord Jesus Christ

Father spoke to me about holding a revival at the church for forty days. So I went into a fast and prayer and went to Tana's aunt and uncle to see what they thought. They were all for it, so we set the dates, got information out, and was ready to go. We started the meetings in the summer of 1996. During the first couple of weeks, things went great, people were showing up, Father was moving, and we were on the verge of something big happening— much like we had seen at the church we were at before we came here. I was ready; then, right out of the pan into the fire we went. Certain people didn't like what was going on; the pastors listened and started finding fault. Then, it happened again; they asked us to leave because they didn't want that kind of stuff going on in their church. So here we were again, thrust back into the wilderness. By this time, I was done trying to get anything done with people and told Father I would serve him for the rest of my life and do anything he asked as long as I didn't have to deal with people.

I had been either asked to leave or told I didn't belong by seven different churches. Something had to be wrong with me, and I wasn't ministering anymore.

WALKING FURTHER INTO THE WILDERNESS

BY THIS TIME, TANA AND I were both first-degree black belts in what they called taekwondo, our business was still going well, we didn't have a church, and our dreams of ministry were gone. All I could hear Father say was, "Raise your boy to follow me". We went to different churches, tried non-spirit-filled churches, tried all the spirit-filled churches, and none of them seemed right. So we just settled into a Nazarene church with Tana's sister and her husband. They were a loving people and made us feel very welcomed. On April 4, 1999, we went to resurrection sunday service. As the service went on, Jesse, being only three days away from his fourth birthday, looked up at me and said, "Daddy I want to be saved." My heart melted, and I explained Romans 10:9 and 10: "If you confess with your mouth and believe in your heart that Jesus was raised from the dead, you shall be saved." He understood, and I had the privilege of leading my own son to Jesus Christ as his Lord and Savior right there in the pew on Sunday morning. This was one of the greatest moments of my life. We were there for a little while and realized this just wasn't going to work. We needed to get Jesse into a church that believed in Holy Ghost, tongue talking, and the moving of Father's presence. I was not being negative at all about where we were at; it just wasn't what we needed to fill us and train Jesse, so we moved on.

I had all this God stuff bottled up inside me and didn't know what to do with it. Off to find a church was the plan. In June of 1999, we went back to a church we had visited a year earlier; it was a Foursquare Gospel Church. I didn't even know there was this kind of church until we visited it. It seemed to have what we thought we needed, so we gave it a try. The first Sunday we were there, I had a Word of the Lord for the pastor, and I thought, *no Lord not today*. So I went to a man that I knew from the past and asked him to help. He went and got the pastor after church. I gave the Word to him, and seven weeks later, it had all come to pass. Then, we just settled in and didn't do anything, began the healing process again.

Our pastor didn't push us, ask questions—anything at all. He just let us come and enjoy services without any pressure. By this time, Jesse was studying martial arts with us and was just having fun. The construction business was still going all right, but my body wasn't holding up, particularly my knees. We had an opportunity to do a "martial arts after school" program, and we started in the fall of 1999. When the spring of 2000 came around, the students didn't want to stop for summer break, so we started our own martial arts school in our basement. In the future, we would go into thirteen different schools and bring many of those students into our home for classes. We had every student learn John 14:6: "And Jesus said I am the Way, the Truth, and the Life and no man come unto the Father except through Me." This was our scripture and still is for the ministry. Martial arts became a huge part of our lives, and even though we used this to spread the gospel, we still let it become consuming in many ways. We started getting so many students that we were busy every night of the week with two to three classes a night. This turned into our business, our livelihood.

We traveled to many tournaments and held two each year ourselves. We traveled to Cancun, Mexico, and competed internationally; Jesse and I became world champions. This was where a prophecy came to pass as we were asked to perform in the opening ceremony. The three of us did musical katas to Christian music in front of seven hundred to eight hundred competitors. All three of us were National Points champions for five years straight and were inducted into the Martial Arts Hall of Fame several times. I became a fifth-degree master black belt in two styles. Tana was a fourth-degree black belt, and Jesse became a third-degree black belt. I had become a certified personal trainer, an aerobics instructor, certified nutritional advisor, a power lifter and body builder. I said all this to show that our wilderness was consumed in our occupation and even though we were using it as an outreach, it was not Father's perfect plan for our life. We substituted worldly activities for the true calling in our lives.

We were attending church but not building a relationship with Father. When Jesse started first grade, he joined Cub Scouts. Tana became a den mother, and halfway through the first year, I got involved. Jesse went on to be a tremendous eagle scout, earning many awards and was being outstanding in everything he did. I became his scoutmaster and excelled in awards and in building a troop. This was also used as an outreach for the kingdom, and we saw fruit—but still not what Father had planned for us. We were in the wilderness yet were enjoying Father's provision. We were still doing things for the Lord but not to the level he had destined us to be in. When Jesse got into high school, he joined band, and for the next four years, we were band parents, witnessed to band members and parents, and were still in the wilderness.

STARTING THE JOURNEY OUT
OF THE WILDERNESS

WE TRULY ENJOYED BEING WITH and raising our son, but we knew we were not fulfilling our purpose and didn't know if we would ever get to do everything Father had ordained us to do. After four years of attending the Foursquare Church we were at, we knew the callings on our life had to be released. There were some factors in the church that had taken place, and Father had spoken to me that I was to be the assisting minister. I put it out of my mind, and then, I was asked to step into that role. In 2005, Father told me to get licensed again. I told him I didn't need a license and that I could do anything he needed me to do without it. He said, "I want you to get a license because of man's rules. There are places I will need you to go that you will need a license to get into." I thought pastor is not going to agree with this, so I went to him and told him what I had heard. And he said, "I have been waiting on you to do this."

During the procedure of obtaining my license, I had to be interviewed by a panel of Foursquare ministers. During this interview, they asked me all sorts of question to make sure I was believing the same way and "to know them that labor among you" (1 Thess. 5:12). One of the ministers asked me what my calling was. I told him I had been an evangelist and had been operating in that calling for several years. He said, "But what are you?" Not really knowing what he was referring to, I once again responded, "I am an evangelist." He then said, very boldly and with authority, "What are you?" By this time, Holy Ghost quickened my spirit, and I knew what he was referring to. I answered and said, "I am a prophet." Now, I want you to understand Foursquare doesn't recognize prophets as being individuals but someone who is taken care of corporately. As soon as I said, "I am a prophet," this ministered said, "That is right, and that is what God made you to be, and don't you ever deny or back away from confessing to anyone what you are. You are a prophet, that's who you are." This changed me from that point on and taught me that no matter what, don't be ashamed of what Father has created and destined you to be. Even through all the mistakes, bad decisions, and failures, I was still who Father had designed me to be. By being washed in the blood of Jesus and forgiven, if I wanted to fulfill that purpose in my life, nothing or no one could stand in the way of who Father had made me to be.

So by October of 2005, I was licensed. We were very busy with life, but I was getting back into the routine of praying and fasting again as well as listening to the voice of Father. In November of 2005, I started a journal of what Father was speaking to me and kept it all documented. By this time, Jesse was showing his potential and was starting to flourish in the Bible. He had started reading his Bible daily and praying regularly. I started praying in the sanctuary almost every day and had some remarkable encounters with Father. This all started as my wife and I were busy with life and raising our son.

We had the opportunity to go to some conventions, and all three of us went on a mission trip to Mexico in 2009. When we came back from the mission trip, we knew in our heart that our assignment in this church was about over, and we just waited until the right timing appeared. I didn't want to make any mistakes this time. I was hoping I had learned from all the other mistakes in the past.

ON TO A NEW ADVENTURE

BY THE TIME SUMMER OF 2010 came around, we knew it was time and pretty well knew where we were going. So we met with the pastor of another Foursquare Church in our town because to keep my license, I had to have an appointment in a Foursquare Church. We knew Father was going to have to arrange this, and we believed it was time. The next step was to talk to our pastor to see if he would release us. We went in for a meeting and told him we felt it was time for us to leave and that Father was calling us to go help another pastor in town. He told us he hated to see us leave, but he agreed and released us with his blessings. The next Sunday, in August of 2010, we were at the other church, and I was set in as an assisting minister to do evangelistic work out of the church.

There was a lot for us to do, and we were excited to get started. We took over the mission fund which was one Sunday a month, started getting greeters for the morning services, and eventually helped get security set up. The one thing that changed everything was when our pastor asked us to get involved with the other ministers in town because she didn't have the time, and this would keep her in touch with what was going on in our community. This was when the great adventure of our lives began; we just didn't know it yet.

At this time, we didn't see a lot of the manifestations of Father's presence, and we were so hungry to see at least what we had witnessed in the past. But not even that was going on. At the same time we changed churches, in August of 2010, Outpouring services started at Cross Tabernacle Assembly of God Church right here in Terre Haute. I started attending the pastor meetings, which were two—one for those in the southern end of town and the other in the northern end of town. I went to the one in the southern end to begin with. Once a month, they joined together and had a meeting of all of them. At the first one of them I went to, I met a gentleman by the name of Michael Livengood. We prayed together that day and really hit it off. Later, I would find out he was the evangelist for the Outpouring services and had been involved in the big move of God in Pinnsacola, Florida plus a mighty move of God in Hut Valley, New Zealand.

Just about this same time, there was a group of spirit-filled pastors that were meeting at the local International House of Prayer once a week for prayer. I had been invited by a pastor at the south pastor's prayer meeting to attend that. So I went to see what was going on and if it might be something I wanted to get involved in. The group was not very large, but the prayer was intense; and the ministry to each other was off the chart. They prayed in tongues and prophesied over each other, shared and prayed for each other with compassion. At this meeting, I met several men that I would become very close to in the future but one stood out, someone I had been told negative things about in the past but had never met in person. He was the pastor of Cross Tabernacle, Keith Taylor. The next thing I did was to go to an Outpouring service to see what was going on there, and what I found interested me a lot. After going to the prayer meetings for a while and Tana hearing everything going on, she decided to go to see what all the fuss was about. She too was overwhelmed with the presence of Father and started coming regularly. Then, she started attending Outpouring with me. We started out sitting in the back, wondering if this was the genuine thing or not; but after a few times, we came up front to sit, so we wouldn't miss anything. My relationship with Michael Livengood continued to grow, and it didn't take very long for Michael and Keith to recognize the prophetic call in my life. The Outpouring services were normally on Friday evenings, sometimes on Sunday evening, which didn't affect our own church services. For the first year, Michael just would not let go of me. He kept after me to get more involved, and we did.

During this first year, we had a lot of adjusting to do, and what we were experiencing was fabulous. It was great to be in the presence of God, but it still wasn't as strong as what we had seen in the past. The Thursday morning prayer group got stronger and stronger as we went, with the fivefold ministry—as mentioned in Ephesians 4:11—rising to the surface and taking its place in the group. There was something different about this group, and we knew we were exactly where Father wanted us at this time in our lives.

Meanwhile, in our own church, things were going great, and we were enjoying serving and developing relationships in the Foursquare Church. On October 26, 2010, we attended the Heartland District Foursquare Convention; this was when I was ordained into the Foursquare International Church. We also got opportunities to start ministering and started doing a little traveling. Scouting was still a big part of our life, and Jesse was working on his eagle scout project. The martial arts school was our source of income, so we had to stay close to home to keep classes going. But what we experienced in this year was enough to make us want more of God than ever before. To say the least, this first year after changing churches, meeting a group of ministers that were interested in who I was and the calling in my life, getting involved in Outpouring services, and enjoying church again was a big change in atmosphere for us. And we decided there was no going back to the old way of church ever again. On to the Promise Land.

THE THIRD MAN

BEFORE WE GET STARTED ON this, let's take a look at just what has gone on in my life. There were the mistakes I had made, yet Father was still willing to use this ignorant and unlearned man who had been asked to leave seven churches, filed bankruptcy twice, had an affair, been divorced, and just messed up in so many ways. In October of 2008, my dad died. In August of 2009, my brother-in-law died at sixty-five years old. In 2010, my wife's brother fell off the side of a barn and was paralyzed from the chest down. And I had dealt with some serious physical problems—a modern-day David, a complete screw up that shouldn't have any chance at all for God to want or even consider using in ministry. Yet here I was in the middle of a move of God that looked to be bigger than what happened in Florida. Only through the grace and mercy, repentance, forgiveness and washing in the blood of my Savior, Jesus Christ, could the prophetic words that had been spoken come to pass and the purpose Father had for my life be fulfilled. The men that Father had put me with believed in Tana and I, recognized our callings, and encouraged us to move on in them. By the fall of 2011, we had been asked to be a part of the ministerial team of the Outpouring services. We were being used in ministering at the altar. I was giving prophetic words and was being included in everything going on.

Then, a man came to speak at the Outpouring service in October of 2011. He was a close friend of Michael and was the assisting pastor of the church that Michael was with in New Zealand. He was a very ordinary man with an extraordinary presence of God around him. His name was Graham Renouf and, unknown to me, would become very important in my walk with God. He carried a glory of God, and it manifested as drunkenness in the physical. This is spoken of in the Bible in Acts 2:15, where it says, "For these are not drunken as ye suppose, seeing it is but the third hour of the day." I had experienced this type of thing at a Full Gospel Businessmen's Convention in Owensboro, Kentucky, years back in my first marriage. I went out in the Spirit and stayed on the floor for hours, and when they did get me up, I was so drunk I couldn't sit in a chair or walk. I stayed that was all night and finally got back to what I thought was normal the next day. But this was something beyond what I had experienced and with more purpose.

I watched him closely, studied the way he ministered, and examined everything he said and did. I was fascinated by how God used him, and he was just an ordinary person—as common as I was—yet there was such a presence of Father; I wanted what he had and more. We had a meeting at the local International House of Prayer. Graham was there, and he ministered to me and prophesied over Tana and I. He told me I would raise the dead, not just the spiritually dead but also the physically dead. This would be the first of many words he would speak into my life. As you will see, even though he lived on the other side of the world, he became a big part of the life. Graham seemed to have an infectious way about him, and when I would get close, the drunkenness would affect me. And it definitely had an effect on Pastor Keith. All he would have to do, and still do, is to say, "Have another drink, mate." And the presence of God would hit. There will be a lot more about Graham in the future.

Now, there were three major players in my life—men of God that didn't care about the mistakes I had made in the past, saw the calling in my life, and was encouraging me to fulfill that calling. At the prayer meeting on Thursday morning, I gave a Word of the Lord to Graham. Yes, that is right. Father had me, of all people, give a Word to this man of God. I wasn't too comfortable with that, but the way it turned out, it was Father establishing relationship. Now, I had Evangelist/Teacher Michael Livengood, who grabbed a hold of me like a bulldog and wouldn't let go; Apostle Keith Taylor, who I learned to trust and confide in about everything; and Prophet Graham Renouf, who could read your mail—what a trio of men Father had placed in my life. Never before in all my life did I have this kind of relationships with those I trusted and that cared for me for who God had purposed me to be—men I trusted to speak into my life and also guide me through the mistakes by correction. But Father always has more.

MORE RELATIONSHIPS
AND STORIES

WE WERE OVER A YEAR into these Outpouring services, and many manifestations of the presence of God were showing up. I seemed to find myself, during the altar time, out in the congregation, ministering to people mostly to receive the baptism in Holy Ghost. On one of these times, I was assisting a young lady, and she received her prayer language; everything was great. As I was starting to move away, the young lady's grandmother said, "You have gold dust on you." I said, "What?" And she repeated herself. Sure enough, I looked on my shoulders, having on a dark shirt, and there was gold dust. Then I looked at my hands, and there it was on my hands. I had never seen this or heard of it before. It was so cool. My son came over to me and was trying to scrape it off, so he could have some. Some would say, "Where is this in scripture?" And I say they prayed in Acts 4:30 for signs and wonders, and this was a wonder. I realized just how much we limit God because of our religious thinking. I was so excited and went to tell Apostle Keith. When I explained to him what went on, he said, "Oh, we find that upstairs in the balcony on the carpet all the time." Boy, where have I been? I came to find out this type of manifestation had showed up at other moves of God in the past. I just had never heard of it. This continued to happen around me for several months as it would appear on people I was praying for or on me. You never knew when it would happen, but it was sure neat to see it.

We had been invited to a meeting on New Year's Eve to usher in the year of 2012. We decided to go. It was in a house in the country; there was a good group of people there in a big house. We didn't know anyone there except the person who had invited us, and he didn't show up until later in the evening. We visited with everyone, and I started hearing Father's voice. And I knew he was going to want me to speak into some of their lives. The evening went on, and there was a young woman that seemed to be in charge as well as an older gentleman they were all looking to for guidance. The gentleman that had invited us finally showed up, and we were already into the service. Several different people spoke, and finally, the older gentleman was given control of the meeting. There was a humbleness about him, yet he took authority over the meeting and the direction it was going. They were calling him Apostle Z; I came to find out his name was Ronald Zimmmerman. When things were coming to a close, Father said, "Speak now." I argued with him about it, but that didn't do any good; and so I asked if they would be willing for me to speak, and they said yes. I thought, *why are you having me to do this?* But I was obedient. So I spoke into Apostle Z's life and into the young lady that was in charge. This was all so we could start new relationships, and Brother Z, as I call him, had become a very important person in my life.

As the Outpouring services kept going, the more I was being used, the more I continued to lead people into the baptism of Holy Spirit. There were pastors coming from all over to be a part of what was going on. One of these pastors came because he was on the verge of giving up and didn't know what to do. He came to the Outpouring, and his whole life changed from being in the presence of God. He went back to his church, totally changed everything, and his church had a complete turnaround. He wrote a book about his experience, *River Rising*, a great book about what Father is doing in his body today.

The Outpouring started to spread to other churches, and we went to another town where Apostle Keith was ministering. We saw Father move there, but the big thing that happened for us was Jesse, our son, seemed to have a tremendous breakthrough in ministry while we were there. Things in our own church were going well, but we knew there was more; we had not seen the power of God. We had seen salvations, deliverances, healing, drunkenness, laughter, glory clouds, and baptism in Holy Ghost, but we knew there was more. In October of 2012, we attended the Foursquare Heartland District Convention held in Michigan. Things seemed to really break loose for us, and we had a great time meeting lots of new people and contacts for ministry.

In November, Graham came back to minister again. It is always so much fun to be around Graham, and we were invited to go out to eat with Michael Livengood and his wife, Linda, and Graham and his wife, Linda, to Olive

Garden. The waitress seated us in the middle of the room on a hardwood floor in chairs that had rollers. I went in and sat down beside Graham; and he reached over, slapped me on the back, and said, "Have another drink, mate." Instantly, we were both drunk in the Spirit in the middle of Olive Garden. Every time we would lean forward, it would push our chairs away from the table. The other four sitting there with us just laughed and watched as we kept trying to act normal, rolling back and forth away from the table. Boy, it was hard to eat spaghetti.

Tana had finally decided to get her minister's license, and our pastor at our home church encouraged her. And on December 24, 2012, she received her license. I was so proud of her and knew all along she was to get them, but it was all the timing of it that had to take place. By this time, we knew Father was calling us into full-time ministry. Our martial arts school had dwindled down to three students, so we decided to not take on any new students and try to get these three as far as we could in the next year. On December 31, 2012, I officially retired from being scoutmaster of Troop 30. All things were falling in line; now, we had to trust in Father to keep us. During this last year, several opportunities had opened up for us to minister, and Father was anointing us to lead people in the baptism of Holy Ghost. The Words of the Lord were flowing, and ministry had really become fun.

TAKING TIME TO LOOK BACK

BEFORE WE GO ON WITH the next big change in my life, I would like to look back on some of the things that took place spiritually that haven't been mentioned yet. It's not like I didn't see God through my life, and I want to share some of those times when I knew I was in the palm of his hand. Here are a few things that happened.

Weather always seemed to be an area that I dealt with. At least four times, I survived a tornado. Once on a ball field with no ditches to get in, I just lay on the ground and prayed. The tornado was off the ground up in the sky; I could see it and feel it pulling me up. It hit two miles away in a wooded area. The next one, I was in a car headed for work. I pulled out onto the highway, couldn't see anything but a wall of water, and prayed in the name of Jesus. It went two blocks behind me down the middle of town where I had just come from. The car was being tipped up on its side, then back down. The third one I saw coming across a field. I was trying to get my car windows rolled up, gave up, ran in the house calling out the name of Jesus, couldn't get the door to closed because of the vacuum, got my wife into a closet as it took roofing and the chimney off the house, jumped over our horse lot, and hit a grove of trees one hundred yards down the road. On the fourth one, we were horse camping at a state park. The storm moved in, and we knew it was a bad one. Just like the others, I prayed and commanded it to go in the name of Jesus. We had hail, wind, and rain, but what we didn't know until after everything ended was what the Rangers said. It was like the tornado split in two, went on both sides of the camp area, then rejoined back together on the other side. Everything was so torn up we couldn't ride the trails and had to go home. This same thing happened again years later on a camping trip with my scout troop. A severe storm was coming in from the northwest headed right for us. We were in a Boy Scout Campground for summer camp. I had the boys start praying and got out in the open and started rebuking it. I then walked up to the camp office, which was about half a mile away. When I got up there, they said, "You are not going to believe this." They showed me on radar that the storm was coming right toward us, split in two, and went in two different directions, not hitting us at all. Jesus taught us to do this by example in Luke 8: 22–25.

Many times, lightning has struck close to where I had been but sometimes, very close. One time, when I was a little boy, it was raining very hard, and I was playing in the rain and water at my grandma's. They had us come in and just when we got on the porch, a bolt of lightning struck a tree close to the house, and the water on the ground where I had been playing glowed. Another time, I was painting inside this big old home that was empty. I had a ladder leaning up against the wall; it was summer time, so I had all the windows open. It had started storming; I continued

58

to paint when a lightning bolt struck a tree just outside the window. A ball of fire flew through the window under the ladder I was on and out the other window. It shook the whole house. After I checked my pants, I went to see what it had hit. The tree had all its bark blown off—the craziest thing I had ever seen. It was even on the news with pictures of what it had done. I was in a poll barn where we kept our horses, cleaning out stalls when lightning hit a lightning rod on top of the barn. The sound was deafening; the whole end of the barn lit up with an orange glow. Father's protective hand has been around me all my life. He is the reason I don't fear nature because he has his hand over me.

Unexplainable Occurrences

One of the times, we were horse camping. It was hot, so we decided to go swimming in one of the strip pits. We loaded into the truck and, as soon as we got there, ran, and dove into the pit. We stayed for an hour or so, then loaded up and went back to camp. When we got back, I realized I didn't have my glasses. I looked everywhere, then remembered I had them on when we went. I got to thinking, and it hit me. I had dove into the water with them on. I went back to where we had been, praying all the way there.

When I didn't see them on the bank, I determined about where I had dove into the water and started wading out. Three passes in water neck deep, I felt them with my foot. That is only God that can do that. This happened with an ax head in 2 Kings 6—only, the axe head floated.

While I was working in the factory on the receiving end of a big machine, I heard someone say my name. I thought it was the operator, so I went around to see what he wanted. He said he didn't call, so I went back. Pretty soon, I heard it again, an audible voice. I could see the operator; I knew it wasn't him, but there was no one else around. So like Samuel in the Old Testament, I waited to hear it again; and sure enough, God spoke to me again, and I responded. He fellowshipped with me in the Spirit during the biggest part of the shift of work. What a wonderful experience.

I had gotten ready and went on to bed that evening before my wife, my first wife. I was in bed, praying, and I sensed a presence; and I smelled an aroma like I had never smelled before. I was lying on my stomach; and I never rolled over, for I knew Jesus was walking through my bedroom. And that sweet aroma was so awesome. I have never forgotten that smell and have had the privilege of smelling other times since then. I wish I had looked to see him, but it was like I was overwhelmed by his presence.

I was at a Full Gospel Businessmen's Conference in Owensboro, Kentucky. The speaker was great, and afterward, I went forward for prayer. When I got prayed for, I went down in the Spirit. I was down for a long time; they even cleaned up and swept the floor around me. They sat me up in a chair, but I fell off of it. I was so drunk I couldn't walk. They helped me the rest of the evening, and I was still drunk the next morning. What an encounter—but nothing like something that would happen years later.

One time, I came out of church, went to my car, and found a typed out letter from Jesus on the driver's seat. The car was locked, and no one had a key but me. The letter was one of encouragement and love, something I really needed at that time, and there was no explanation of how it got there.

I will never forget the time I was in my church, praying during the day—something I had been doing for weeks—and I sat down in front of the pulpit. Only a few of the lights were on, but all of a sudden, it was like lights started shining from on the stage out toward the seats. Then, I saw this shadow coming from behind the pulpit. It startled me at first, then a wonderful peace came upon me. The light was very bright, and the shadow covered me. Holy Spirit spoke to me and said, "This is what I mean by being in the shadow of the Almighty." You are out front doing what you are supposed to be doing, but no one can see you because of the brightness of the glory.

Miracles

The event of raising the dead woman that I had in the Philippines, when she had an out-of-body experience, was not the first time I had raised the dead. I was in the barn one day. One of our horses had gotten sick, and I was giving the horse two shots of penicillin a day. This was to be done for a week. The horse was a fifteen-hands-high Quarter Horse; I gave him the shot. He started shaking, eyes rolled back in his head, and dropped like a lead balloon. My first wife went nuts; this was her horse. I told her to call the vet and see what we were to do. I started praying and trying to see if he was breathing. Nothing, he had just dropped dead on the spot. My wife went in to call the vet, and I started screaming life back into his body, at the top of my lungs. She came back out crying and said he was going to call back. I said go back into the house and wait on the call. She did, and he did and tell her it sounded like a reaction, and for him to live, it would take an injection to counteract the reaction, but there was no way of getting there in time. If he was on the ground, there was nothing that could be done. By this time, I had gotten mad and started commanding that horse to live in the name of Jesus Christ and slapped him on the chest. He took a big breath and started thrashing around; I got out of the stall. He did everything but tear the barn down, getting out of that stall. He got out into the lot and started running as hard as he could for at least fifteen minutes. I told my wife to call the vet and see what we were to do now. She did; he said he didn't know. The horse should be dead. The horse had been on the ground not breathing for over twenty minutes. There was no explanation why he got up—only the power and life in the name of Jesus Christ.

I had a friend that had an accident which left him without the use of his legs. I spent a lot of time with him, praying for him and taking care of him. I had carried him into the living room of the house he was staying at, set him in a chair, and commanded him to walk in the name of Jesus. Nothing happened, so I went over and sat down in a chair and started singing and praising God. When I looked up, he was standing to his feet—completely healed, all in the name of Jesus.

During a revival that we saw many things happen, a friend of mine was there. He had been involved in a factory accident and caught in a machine that almost tore him in two. This accident had caused a lot of internal damage and left him in pain all the time. He came forward for prayer.

Holy Spirit moved, the power of God fell on him, and he was instantly healed—to God be all the glory.

We were at church one Sunday morning, and there was a six-year-old boy there with his grandma. They told me he had been told by the doctors that he had a bad heart and would have to be operated on and wanted me to pray for him. So I did; all I said was, "Be healed in the name of Jesus." The little boy turned to his grandma and said, "I'm healed." They had a doctor's appointment the next week, and when the doctors examined him, they could find nothing wrong anywhere. My God can do anything.

I was ministering at a small church where my wife's grandparents had helped start the church. There were several things that had happened that night, and this lady blurted out, "I need prayer. I just came from the hospital, so I could be here tonight." I came to find out she had cancer in her stomach, and it didn't look good in the natural. We had seen a couple of people already healed that evening, so I told my wife to lay her hand on the lady's stomach. And I just prayed, "Be healed in Jesus's Name." The lady screamed and said, "Fire just went through my stomach." She went back to the doctor the next week, and the doctor said she was healed.

In the same church on a Sunday morning, a lady asked for prayer for her hands. she had arthritis, and her fingers were all distorted. I prayed, "In the name of Jesus, be healed." And her fingers straightened out and was healed.

It would take another book to write all the stories of how Father has healed me personally. Father doesn't always heal you the way you think he would. One of those times was when I was playing basketball, and I twisted my ankle really bad. It swelled instantly and turned black within minutes. After I was done rolling around on the ground in pain, I finally said, "Father, heal this ankle in the name of Jesus." I had a friend get me to my feet, and I just kept saying, "Ankle, you are healed in the name of Jesus." From that point on, the pain went away but the swelling and the color stayed. I walked on it, ran on it—no pain. Father healed it, but with the physical eye, you could not tell, except I was not limping.

Angels and Demons

Now, don't let me lose you here. The thing about a testimony is that even when others may question you on whether it is the truth or not, no one can change your mind when you are the one who experienced it, saw it with your own eyes. For some reason, Father lets people see into the spirit world—when he chooses to do so. Here are some of those times in my life. Angels and demons are seen throughout the Bible.

I was mowing grass at the place we were renting; I can't say I was even praying or even thinking about anything spiritual. I looked up, and at the corner of the land we had, I saw this angel as big as the trees with his sword drawn. He didn't look like he was paying any attention to me; he was just standing there. Then, I looked around, and on every corner of this five-acre plot of land, there was one of these angels. I just stood there, and Father spoke to me and said, "You are guarded, don't worry about it." I stood there for a while longer, and it was like they just faded away. I praised God and finished mowing my grass. I never saw them again. I did keep looking though.

I was in a church service, and the lights were turned down. When I looked up on the platform, there was this figure, bigger than a normal man, watching like he was studying what was going on. When I closed my eyes, I could still see this figure just like when I had my eyes open. I kept looking, he didn't have wings, but his countenance was holy and pure. I watched him for a good little while, and then, I couldn't see him anymore. I will tell more about angels later—now, my encounters with demons.

Shortly after I was baptized in Holy Spirit, I held a revival in a small town in a neighboring county. It was to go for a week but ended up staying for two weeks. On the first week, I went to the church to pray during the day. When I walked in, I had this creepy feeling come all over me. I walked into the sanctuary, and up on the wall just under the ceiling were these distorted-looking monkey type beings. I started praying in the Spirit; they acted like they didn't think I could see them. As Holy Spirit directed, I pointed right at each one and commanded it in the name of Jesus to leave. Every time I said the name of Jesus, the one I was pointing at disappeared and left the building.

Going back to a story I told earlier, when I was with a friend that had lost the use of his legs, just before his miracle happened, he was lying in the bed, and there were two demons, one setting on each shoulder dressed in tuxedos. They were three to four inches tall. Holy Spirit told me to command them to leave in the name of Jesus and to return to the post they came from. I did; they did and went into the fence post outside. Don't ask me; I just did what I was told.

I went to a meeting, where a man known for his deliverance ministry was speaking and ministering. The night before, he had asked everyone to bring anyone they knew who had a demon and wanted delivered. So when I went, I was expecting to see something; well, I did. When the ministering time came, and they started praying, casting the demons out of the people. I could hear them screeching through the air as they came out of the people. I wanted to see more, so I went forward to be of assistance and so I could be closer to what was going on. Those demons would throw the people on the floor to keep them from casting them out, and the people ministering would go after them. I wasn't seeing anything, only the manifestation of the demons in the physical actions of those needing delivered. Things were calming down when I noticed this one man on the floor with a man on each arm and each leg and one sitting on his chest. Then, the one being held down just sat up like no one had a hold of him. They got him back down. There was one guy who was trying to cast it out but wasn't having any success. The gentleman that was there ministering was sitting in a chair on the stage, watching all this go on. He told the guy who was trying to cast the demon out to get up and stop. Then, he looked at me and said, "You." I looked around and said, "Me?" He said, "Yes, cast it out." Now, I had dealt with demons before but not on this scale. But I thought no demon in hell is bigger than the name of Jesus, so I got down beside the guy and started commanding the thing to come out in the name of Jesus. It took about ten minutes. When his eyes rolled back, he screamed, he threw up this terrible smelling green slime, trying to make sure he hit me, then went completely limp.

When he came around, he was normal and remembered nothing that went on.

A guy who I had started working with moved into a house down in the river bottoms. The place had been used to do some satanic worship and sacrifices, but he didn't know this till later. I got a call one evening just a few days before we were leaving to go to the Philippines on a missionary trip. His wife was in a panic. She said he was growling like a dog, and she didn't know what to do. So my wife and I went to see what needed to be done. When we got there, he was on the couch on his hands and knees, growling like a dog. His wife and children were on the other side of the room, terrified. I told Tana to get them into the other room and started ministering. I asked to speak to the man in the name of Jesus and called him by name. His eyes rolled back to normal, and he spoke to me. I asked him if he wanted delivered and he said, "Yes, help me." As soon as he said yes, the thing took back control and acted like it was going to attack. I continued to speak the name of Jesus. This went on about half an hour. Finally, I got an authority that raised up in me and commanded it to leave. He jumped up, grabbed a hide a bed couch, lifted it up above his head, came right at me, and threw it. It was like it hit a force field and fell straight down about three feet in front of me. He then jumped up on the couch he had just threw at me and rose up like he was going to attack me. When he did, his arm was hit by a ceiling fan. He grabbed the fan and pulled it out of the ceiling, then jumped off the couch and ran outside. I quickly followed him out. When I got outside, he was lying on the porch in his right mind and asking what had happened. I held him and told him we would talk later. We then cleansed the house, casting and running out all demons in Jesus's name. We used a lot of oil, and they never had any trouble after that.

Transported

On two different times while traveling to Indianapolis, Indiana from Terre Haute Indiana, Tana and I were transported. The first time was about twenty miles of distance from the time we were in one spot to the next thing we knew we were at another spot. The second time, it was about a sixty-mile difference, and there was no time lapse. And we had no recall of how we got to where we were.

One time, coming home from Marshall, Illinois, to Terre Haute, Indiana, I had this happen, and I was at my turn off, once again with no time lapse. Tana and Jesse were traveling down Twenty-Fifth Street and was transported six blocks. They both looked at each other and realized what had happened. For whatever reason, these occurrences happened, and we praise Father for his protective hand. I wanted to share these things to show the grace and mercy of Father and how much he loves even those who make mistakes and fall short but are willing to repent and ask forgiveness. I could keep on going but I think you get the idea that Father can use anyone, even an ignorant and unlearned man.

BIG CHANGES GOOD AND BAD

THIS NEXT YEAR WOULD TURN out to be a year of traveling more, which was a good thing and something we enjoy but also a time period of great challenges as we started to draw even closer to Father in our personal walks. So much happened, and to get it all in order probably will not take place. Shortly after the beginning of the year in 2013 on January 18, we had an Outpouring service at Cross Tabernacle Church. The speaker was Seth Fawcet, Graham Renouf's pastor from New Zealand. This was the first and only time to this point that I have ever seen him. He started ministering that night, and the presence of Father was really strong. He was very saturated with Holy Spirit and what we call drunk in the Spirit. This is when the presence of God is so thick that you literally feel and act drunk but it is a spiritual condition. I was fascinated with this because I had experienced this before in my life but not to the extent I was seeing through Apostle Seth. I decided I wanted to see this closer, so as he started moving through the sea of people, ministering to them, I placed myself as close to him as I could—following him around, watching as he would point his finger at people, shoot like a gun, and they would fall under the power of the Holy Ghost. He was so drunk in the Spirit it took two men to hold him up, and he just kept ministering. It was so neat to watch, and I wondered what that would be like to minister in that way. We went on with the service, and finally, they said they wanted all the five-fold ministers to come up on the stage. There were over fifty of us that went up and were standing as Apostle Seth started laying hands on different ones. I was standing at the opposite end from where he started ministering and was just asking Father to do with me whatever he wanted. As far as I know, before Apostle Seth ever got to me, I went down on the floor, slain in the Spirit, on the stage with a live stream on the Internet. I don't remember anything else that happened for a good hour and a half; I was just enjoying the presence of Father in a way I had never experienced before. They just left me lying there on the stage and went on with the service. With me being under the lights shining on the stage, my wife said I looked like a corpse. When everything was done and people were beginning to leave, I started to come around but something wasn't the same. They tried to get me up, but I didn't have any control. I was so drunk in the Spirit I couldn't even stand. They sat me in a chair, and I fell out of the chair at least three times. Finally, they got a couple of guys to literally pick me up, so they could get me out of the building and to my van. Jesse drove home because I could not function. Tana and Jesse finally got me into the house and into bed. I woke up the next morning still drunk, stumbling around the house, bouncing off walls. I couldn't talk right; I was wrecked big time. I stayed this way for five days, unable to do anything because of being so drunk in the Spirit of the Lord. This experience proved to be a life-changing event, and I have never been the same since. It changed the way I looked at things. I became funny to be around and funny to watch. My ministering changed, and you never knew what I was going to say or do. From this point on, I started getting drunk in the Spirit anytime, anywhere as Holy Spirit wanted. I am talking in gas stations, grocery stores, clothing stores, on the street, and anytime we went into a church. Most of the time, I am drunk before I get out of the van in the parking lot of the church and stay that way till I get home. When I go to minister, I have to be helped up to the stand and make sure I have something to hang on to. But the one thing that happened was we saw more salvations, baptisms in Holy Ghost, instant healings, deliverances, and the Word of the Lord just flowed. I was messed up and finally out of the way so Father could do whatever he wanted to with me.

Shortly after this—the last of February and the first of March—I started having some physical problems. I had a full checkup in November of 2012, and everything was fine. But when I went to find out what was wrong, they told me I had diabetes. It was like my pancreas just quit working. What a blow. They tried pills, and that didn't seem to even phase it; so they started me on shots, but the doctor really thought I would have to on a pump. I told the doctor my Father had healed this, and I was healed. I truly believed this would be a very short attack of the enemy, and I would have a tremendous testimony. Well I do have a tremendous testimony, but things haven't went the way I had planned. I am still dealing with this. But I know Jesus is my healer, and I will never say otherwise.

LEARNING TO LIVE LIFE AS
A HOLY GHOSTAHOLIC

LET ME BACK UP JUST a bit. I started 2013 on a fast, and it was the twelfth day of the fast that my drunk experience happened. On the next day, we had nine boys from Jesse's Bible club at school come over to have fellowship. Here I was, drunk in the Spirit. All kinds of things went on. One had a vision, two were baptized in Holy Spirit, and one was slain in the Spirit. These kids were from all kinds of church backgrounds.

Then, on the first weekend in February, we went to Oshkosh, Wisconsin, to minister for the weekend. We saw two receive Jesus as Savior, five baptized in Holy Ghost, several healings, and multiple Words of the Lord. Then, we started seeing supernatural manifestations occurring. During an Outpouring service, I was standing, worshiping, and I noticed my hands were wet. Now, I sweat a lot, but this was different. Oil started forming on my hands, and to the point, it dripped off of my hands. I showed it to Michael Livengood and others, and they had me start laying hands on people. That was really neat. We started seeing many instant healings, and it became very easy to lead someone in the baptism of Holy Ghost.

On March 13, I had another encounter with Father and was out on the floor for two hours. On March 22, oil and gold dust showed up on my hands. This time, when I laid hands on people, they were healed. One man received his sight, a woman's neck was healed, kidney stone pain was instantly gone, and more. In the middle of April, we made another trip to Oshkosh, Wisconsin, and we saw more of the same—all kinds of healings, filled with Holy Ghost and the prophetic, flowing like a river. Then, at another Outpouring service, oil showed up on my hands again. A lady dropped her crutches and took off around the church, and a nine-year-old got baptized in Holy Ghost. By this time, I am known as the drunken prophet because I am always drunk in the Spirit.

COULD WE BE PASTORS?

IN MAY OF 2013, APOSTLE Keith came to us and asked if we would be interested in becoming pastors of a small church in Clay City, Indiana. I had never thought I had been called to be a pastor, but I told him I would be willing to go and fill in till they got someone—with the agreement that if Father asked us to take it as pastors we would. This was the catch to the whole thing, Tana's grandmother and grandfather, her two sisters, their husbands, and three other people started and founded this church in 1927. Her grandfather was helping build the fellowship hall at the time he died. There was a lot of heritage there, and we didn't know exactly what Father wanted us to do. There were two other guys Apostle Keith was sending down there, and we were taking turns filling in on Sundays. The church membership was down to eleven, only eight were still attending, and normally, not over five showed up any given Sunday. They didn't have Sunday evening service and no midweek service. It was run by two older ladies, who took care of everything.

Before he resigned, we had met the pastor of this church at an Outpouring service. Because of meeting him and our connection to the church, Tana had started stopping by the church, anointing it with oil and praying over it as she traveled to help take care of her dad once a week in Linton, Indiana. Sometimes, I would go with her and pray. On one of these occasions, after Apostle Keith had asked us to consider taking the church, we were walking the property and praying. I looked up above the church and saw this huge angel standing on the roof. He had a sword in his hand, and it was like he was standing guard. As I looked at him, he looked down at me and said, "I've got your back," then looked back up. After this happened, Tana and I started wondering if being the pastors of this church was what Father wanted us to do. I was not in favor of the idea, at all, but was willing, I thought, to go ahead. There was a lot more to Father's plan that I knew nothing about, and why did that angel say what he said?

I figured that as soon as these little old ladies saw me drunk in the Spirit, they would run me out and not want anything to do with us. But the first Sunday we were there, Father opened things up. I started prophesying, drunk in the Spirit, just being me as Father was shaping me to be. When service was over, everyone was happy, and one of the ladies said, "I remember when that happened a lot." I couldn't believe what I was hearing. As I mentioned, there were three of us rotating in the pulpit, and there were also others coming to try out to be pastor.

One Sunday, we came in to minister, and there had been another man that had come the Sunday before to try out. The ones that were there were to vote on the gentleman to see if they wanted him. I found out right before service that my name was also going to be on the ballot.

I told them not to put me on just vote on the one. They voted him in, then he refused and didn't take it.

We filled in a total of seven times over the next few months. We walked the streets of the little town passing out flyers, spent hours praying in the church, and started loving the people. I finally came to the point that I was truly willing to be the pastor of this church, and on my last Sunday morning, Father spoke to Tana and me and said, "This is not where I want you, but you had to be willing to take it. Tana had to come and receive from me what I had for her here from the heritage of her grandparents, the legacy they left here for her." We were released, and Father started really working on the one he had ordained to be there. And it was one of the other two filling in. We established a really good relationship with him and his wife.

GETTING BACK ON COURSE

WHILE WE WERE FILLING IN at the Clay City church, Graham Renouf and his wife Linda came back ministering to us and reaffirming the calling in our lives. Graham was becoming a strong voice of Father in my life and one I trusted. We ministered to other places while we ministered at the little church. It was amazing what Father was doing with us—dozens getting baptized in Holy Ghost, all sorts of healings taking place, legs growing out as back were being healed, and at one Outpouring service, a lady had a huge mass on the side of her neck. She asked me to pray for her. I remembered thinking, "Oh, boy. Father, only you can do something about this," and he did. I placed my hand on the mass and felt it start shrinking, getting smaller and smaller; the lady went crazy. She then asked me to pray for her daughter who wanted to get pregnant and had been told she couldn't. So I did, and within six months, we got word that she was pregnant. Only Father can do these things, especially with an ignorant and unlearned man like me. It doesn't take a great education and a perfect life, just someone willing to admit when he or she is wrong and ask forgiveness, letting the blood of Jesus wash him or her clean. Don't get me wrong, I believe in getting an education, but a willing heart and obedience to Father is what he is looking for.

At this time in August, Father spoke very clear to me that he wanted me to go through a consecration. I was to set myself apart from everything and focus totally on him. I was to take seven days and not be defiled by anything of the world—not to watch or listen to anything, close myself off away from everything. He said, "You will know when to do this, for you will have anointing oil poured on your head." This will be the sign for you. So I started waiting to see when this was going to happen.

Then, we were invited to go to Mississippi to minister. A couple we knew were making regular trips down there to an area they had went to help out after Hurricane Katrina hit. We really wanted to go. and they said come and go with us, so we did. They knew several different pastors and had some places for us to minister. We only went down for a weekend, twelve hours down, twelve hours back. We ministered in two churches and a county jail. We saw twenty-four get baptized in Holy Ghost and several healings. And Words of the Lord flowed. The people were great, and Father blessed them and us. Nine of the twenty-four that got baptized in Holy Ghost were in the county jail.

We came back from that trip, and in the middle of November, we made our third trip to Wisconsin. This too was a weekend, two-day trip. We arrived in Oshkosh, Wisconsin, on Saturday afternoon, preached in a Lutheran church that they let us use for the service, had two instant healings, and over twenty Words of the Lord. I got up the next morning and ministered in an old bank building, really neat: one salvation, one healing, six baptized in Holy Ghost, and several Words of the Lord. You see, these were small groups of believers that were hungry for more of God, and Father was using this simple man to go minister his Word and love them. He will use anyone who is willing to go; just look at what he did with us.

Then, in December, I felt we were to go back to Mississippi. So I talked to a pastor down there, and he wanted us to come and minister. But nothing was real clear about arrangements. We hardly had anything to make the trip, but I just knew we were to go. So on December 27, we took off for Mississippi. Jesse went with us, and we just went by faith. I tried contacting the pastor that was to take care of us but could not reach him, but we kept on traveling. Finally, we realized it wasn't going to happen, and we didn't have the extra money to get a hotel. So we contacted a pastor who we had met the last time we were there, and they arranged for us to stay the night with their daughter and her family. I didn't have any place to minister at the next day because the pastor that was to keep us was where we were to minister. I then called another pastor—we had only met one time—to see when their service started, to have somewhere to go. They told us, and the next morning, we packed up and went to church just to visit. When we got there, the pastor got up and announced that they had a special guest speaker and welcomed us. One got saved, an eleven-year-old's foot was instantly healed, six got baptized in Holy Ghost, and many Words of the Lord came forth. Father is faithful if you will just go and trust him.

We still didn't have a place to stay. Something was said, and a gentleman said, "I am a truck driver. I will be leaving this afternoon and be gone for two weeks, you can stay at my house as long as you want. So we had a place to stay. God is so good. We ended up ministering at Hatiesburg in a home on Monday. Then on Tuesday, New Year's Eve, we ministered at Mt. Olive. After midnight, I started ministering two instant healings, one was a knot on the throat of a two-year-old girl that instantly went away, and the other was a man's back pain was healed. Nine were baptized in Holy Ghost. What a way to kick off the New Year.

We headed home on Sunday, knowing that a bad storm was going through back home. When we left Mississippi, it was 63 degrees when we finally got home there was fourteen inches of snow, and it was -13 degrees. You never know what you are going to run into when following the will of the Lord.

FATHER ROCKS US AGAIN

IN JANUARY OF 2014, WE planned on going to the Road to Glory Conference in Rochelle, Illinois. We made arrangements to stay in a pastor home in that town and to speak in their church before the conference started. We had a great service on that Sunday morning, eight baptized in Holy Ghost and over twenty Words of the Lord. This was something this little church was not used to, and Father rocked them in a good way.

That evening, we went to the church where the conference was being held. The atmosphere was electric, and there was such excitement in the air. There were men and women of God from all over the country that were coming in for this conference, and we got to be a part of it. Many apostles, including Apostle Keith and Evangelist Michael Livengood, plus prophets and pastors represented the whole five-fold ministry. We had been at this church to visit and were familiar with some of the people who went to church there, and we knew several of those who were coming in to minister. I was drunk in the Spirit from the time we got there until we would leave—most of the time, all day long. The teaching and revelation of the Word was off the charts, and we got to be a part of the ministering team at the altar. So much went on Tana and I never were the same.

They had recognized us as prophets and given us the privilege to speak into the lives of the people as we ministered. The conference was only to go until Wednesday, and on Wednesday night, they were having an oil pouring service. But I didn't get oil poured on my head. On that night, I went to minister to this young lady, and before I got to do anything, she went down under the power of the Lord. Well, I had a Word of the Lord for her, but I decided to just wait. I never got back to her, and at the end of the service, they announced that the meetings would be extended two more days. The next day, this young lady came back and brought her husband. I found them before the service and ended up speaking into both their lives. Then, during the ministering time that evening, their two boys were miraculously healed of an incurable disease that was to end their lives by the age of thirteen. We became close friends with this couple and spiritual parents to them. This young woman wrote a book about her boys' miracles, *A Mother's Prayer and God's Miraculous Answer*. The entire week was an incredible encounter with Father and the beginning of a year of the miraculous in the ministry.

Everywhere we went, people were getting baptized in Holy Ghost, and Father was speaking into lives. At two different Outpouring services, gold dust and oil showed up on my hands. We ministered in small churches, but big things kept happening. We would have ten to fifteen people get Holy Ghost at a time. Then, in April, we made another trip to Wisconsin. We saw several salvations, thirty-two baptisms in Holy Ghost, many Words of the Lord; but what started mostly was instant healings. We got to minister to a small group from Green Bay, Wisconsin. Nine instant healings manifested, and they got excited about the presence of God doing the work. Legs grew out, headaches disappeared, back pain left—so much happened and all because of the presence of Father revealed in the place.

We came home from that trip and went to a small church in the neighboring state not too far from home. Once again, people were hungry for God and were expecting him to do something, and he did. Father called out someone with a back problem. A little older lady came forward; I started having a conversation with her. I found out she was a Baptist, and I asked her what she was doing in a Pentecostal church. She said she had come to hear me. I told her Father had something for her and asked her what was wrong. She said her hip and back hurt, so I had her sit in a chair and one leg was an inch shorter. I kept talking to her, and as I did, her leg grew out without anyone praying. The pain was all gone, and she sat there in amazement of what Father had just done. She got up and walked totally pain free.

I then asked if anyone else needed healed of back pain, and an older gentleman sitting toward the back said, "I do." So I stumbled back to him; remember I get drunk every time I minister. I found out he is eighty-four years old, and one leg is two inches shorter than the other. I asked him if he believed God could heal him, and he said yes. As we watched, Father grew that leg out two full inches, and he kept saying I can feel it growing in my hip. Father did it, but I didn't realize what he had done. The gentleman said,

"You don't understand. I was in a car accident and they had to cut two inches of bone out just below my hip and I just felt it grow back." I just about fell over when I heard it and started praising God for what he had done. When you let the glory of God and his presence take over, anything can happen—and usually does.

Everywhere we ministered, there were legs lengthening and backs being healed, along with the other manifestations that we had come to expect. During the summer, things got slow, but no matter where we went, the presence of Father was there. And nothing was impossible. The miracles that I had not seen, other than when we were overseas, are now happening right here.

In August, our spiritual guide, Prophet Graham, came back and was ministering in a church in a town a couple of hours from us with an apostle that we know and loved, so we went to hear him. They were having an oil pouring service, and once again, I didn't get oil poured on my head. Then, during an Outpouring meeting at Cross T a week later, I had been called up on the platform by Apostle Keith to give a Word of the Lord. I was very drunk in the Lord when all of a sudden, Prophet Graham came up to the platform and said, "God has told me to pour oil on your head." So he took a vile of oil and poured it on my head. I had told no one about what Father had said to me except Tana. When that oil hit my head, I was gone. Graham prophesied over me, but I was on the floor, up on the platform, again. The amazing thing was this happened on August 10, 2014, and Father had spoken it to me on August 10, 2013. When I went home, I started my consecration. I didn't leave the house, talk on the phone, watch anything, or go on the computer. I didn't even shave for seven full days. This was a life-changing experience that not only changed me but our whole household.

TRUSTING FATHER EVEN WITH OUR FINANCES

WE HAD SOME TIMES IN our marriage when we seemed to have a little financial security, but then, things would get tough, and we would have to use what we had and for the most part we struggled in the area of finances. Then, in late August of 2014, Father told us to go to Rochelle, Illiois, and on to Clinton, Iowa, for some meetings and to minister. We were pretty much broke, and the van was not running very good at all. But we knew we were to go, so we decided to be obedient and go. We filled the tank up with gas and had forty-two dollars between the two of us. It was a Sunday after church when we left. We knew how long it takes to get there, and we were running about an hour late. We just accepted the idea that we would be late, and we took off. I made sure I didn't speed, and we just enjoyed the trip over; it was about a four-hour ride. We didn't pay a lot of attention to the time until we got closer to the church, then we realized we were going to get there on time. That should not have happened. When they went to take up the offering, Father told me to give twenty dollars of the twenty-two I had on me. I told Tana what Father was asking me to do, and we agreed to be obedient. Then, we met up with a couple that we were going to visit in their house in Iowa. I followed them the next day to their house and realized we had driven all that way and only used a half tank of gas. In the end, we were blessed with a large financial gift. The van was fixed while we were there, and all our food and housing was taken care of. When we got back home, we had money to pay some bills. Provision is nothing for Father as long as you are obedient, but we had a lot more to learn. "But my God shall supply all your need according to his riches in glory by Christ Jesus" (Phil. 4:19).

LET THE HEALINGS AND MIRACLES BEGIN

IN OCTOBER OF 2014, TANA was to be ordained. This was huge for her. She had fought me for years to get licensed, and now, she was being ordained. The ordination was to take place in Madison, Wisconsin, so I made arrangements to minister while we were up that way. We went to Oshkosh, Wisconsin, then to Madison, Wisconsin, for the ordination, then back to Oshkosh, Wisconsin, to Wausau, Wisconsin, to Rochelle, Illinois, back to Oshkosh, Wisconsin, then to Clinton, Iowa and finally to LaClaire, Iowa, and back home. It was a great trip, we ministered in five different small churches—thirty-two people baptized in Holy Ghost, many Words of the Lord, fifteen water baptisms (in a horse trough in a living room), but the thing we noticed most was the instant healings that took place. We saw twenty-one instant healings, all worth sharing about as Father continually was demonstrating his love for his children.

But there was one I want to make sure you hear. Father had manifested many legs growing out, but each time it happened, Tana was either not standing where she could see or she would see the leg short and then the same length but not see it grow. Something always hindered her from actually watching the leg move. We were in Wausau, Wisconsin, I was giving Words of the Lord over people, and I came to this woman, and Father said, "She needs a healing." So I asked her if she needed a healing. She said, "No." So I said, "Yes, you do." She continued to deny it, and finally, she admitted her back hurt; but it was something she just lived with. I had her come to the front. We pulled a chair up and asked her sit down. Sure enough, one leg was an inch shorter than the other. Now, as soon as I had her sit down, Tana sat on the floor right in front of her, held up her feet, and said, "I am not missing this one." I told the people if they wanted to see Father do a miracle, come up and watch. You see, in a small church, everyone knows everyone, and there is no faking this stuff. They all know each other's business. All these children, over twenty of them, came up and sat all around, and then, the adults came up and were watching from behind. The presence of God was so strong, and his glory filled the room. I just kept talking and never prayed, just stepped back and watched my daddy show off. Tana started getting excited as the leg started growing out, reporting a blow-by-blow description. But then, the leg that was growing went past the other leg. Tana went nuts, wondering what Father was going to do. It grew an inch longer than the other leg and stopped. Then, the original longer leg started growing and grew out to match the other leg. One leg grew two inches, and the other grew one inch. The woman got up, walked around—pain totally gone and at least one inch taller. All the time, those children witnessed God do a miracle right before their eyes. They will never be the same, and this is why we need healing, miracles, signs, and wonders to get our young ones to see Father's glory at work. And you will not be able to keep them out of church.

We came back home and had some places to go minister; and everywhere we went, Father's glory came in, and miracles and healings became normal. Ever since going overseas, I felt that this was what was to be going on but had never seen it. This still was not what I expected, for I was longing to witness greater things than Jesus did to manifest everywhere. Jesus told us this would happen in John 14: 12. We went to Columbus, Indiana, had at least sixteen instant healings; to Seelyville, Idiana, ten instant healings; Clay City, Indiana, nine instant healings; Marshall, Illinois, six instant healings—all before the end of the year. Even when we would just go visit, Father would still use us.

ON TO NEW ADVENTURES

WE WERE ABLE TO ENJOY another trip back to Iowa and Northern Illinois in January of 2015, and nothing slowed down. We went to the conference in Rochelle, Illinois—another great move of God.

The last time we were in Wisconsin, a pastor friend of mine suggested that I get a website and Facebook and tell people about what was going on in the ministry. Well, I am not too good with electronics, but with some help from my son and beautiful wife, we got a Facebook page set up, one for each of us and one for Foxes of Fire Ministries. This gave us the ability to share what Father was doing, and the response was amazing. People were actually interested in what Father was doing in the lives of people we minister to. We started sharing the miracles and healings that were taking place, the salvations and baptisms in Holy Ghost, and God's people wanted to hear. I started sharing Words of the Lord that Father had given me in my private time that touched people.

We were in Rennselaer, Indiana, for four nights, saw seventeen instant healings, ten baptisms in Holy Ghost, and dozens of Words of the Lord. One man healed of fibromyalgia. A young girl healed of scoliosis, and her leg grew out. When we ministered in Sidell, Illinois, the presence of God was so strong people just started getting healed with no one praying. Ten all together were healed, including the pastor as we pulled a chair up front and anyone that sat in that chair received healing. One woman's leg grew out, and it was videotaped. The pastor left the chair there for the next two Sundays, and Father continued to move. When we weren't ministering, we started visiting churches. And the same things went on as the pastors would open it up for us to minister. In Seelyville, Indiana, a man's back was healed that had been injured in a car wreck; his boys had never seen him able to touch his toes, and they were in their early teens. Both of them started crying as Father healed their dad. In a small youth group in Linton, Indiana, two received Jesus as Savior and ten baptized in Holy Ghost. We ministered at a Teen Challenge and had one salvation, fourteen baptisms in Holy Ghost, seven instant healings, and Father was reading their mail. In Mt. Carroll, Illinois, healings took place, hips lined up, and pain left. In Niantic, Illinois, a man was healed of allergies instantly. Also, he, his wife, and two of his girls were baptized in Holy Ghost. An older couple was healed in a bowling alley during a wedding reception in Terre Haute, Indiana. A Church of God pastor's leg grew out. His back was healed while at an Assembly of God Church in Clay City with a Foursquare preacher ministering. All this went on between February through May of 2015. What exciting times and all because Father is looking for anyone who is willing to be used and be obedient to his voice no matter how many flaws they have. Believe me, if Father is willing to use this ignorant and unlearned man, he will certainly be willing to use you too. Pray, repent, believe, and obey, then watch what Father has for you to do. This is not the end of my story, more like the beginning, for Father is not done with me yet. And even greater times are coming. Keep chasing after God and understand that Father is bigger than anything you have done and is willing to use you if you are willing to be used. God bless you, and I hope you enjoyed my story. I want to thank my beautiful wife, Tana, for sticking with me and loving me through the last twenty-six years, and I end this not with a period but a semi-colon;

ABOUT THE AUTHOR

James (Jim) Fox is operating in the office of a prophet, has a deep hunger for souls, moves strongly in the healing ministry, and has an anointing to see people baptized in Holy Ghost. Jim and his wife, Tana, are overseers of Foxes of Fire Ministries and minister throughout the Midwest and other countries, witnessing the power and glory of God everywhere they go. They have been married for twenty-six years, have one son, and are currently residing in Terre Haute, Indiana.